Spy on History®

ANNA STRONG AND THE REVOLUTIONARY WAR CULPER SPY RING

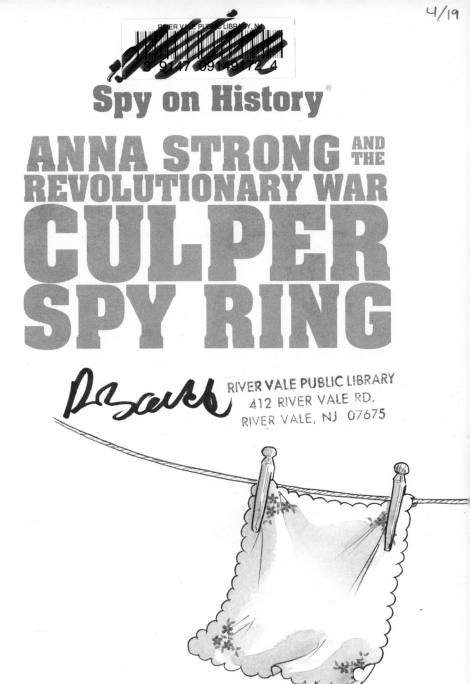

Spy on History®

ANNA STRONG AND THE REVOLUTIONARY WAR CULPER SPY RING

Written by Enigma Alberti
Illustrated by Laura Terry

WORKMAN PUBLISHING
New York

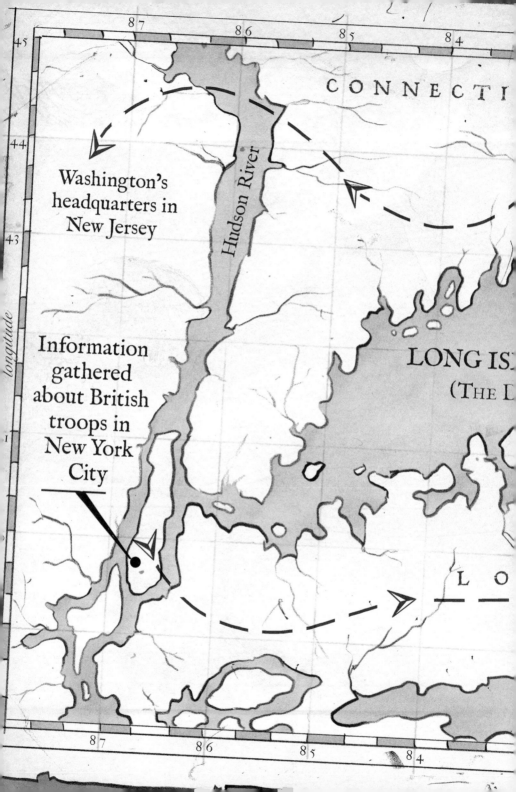

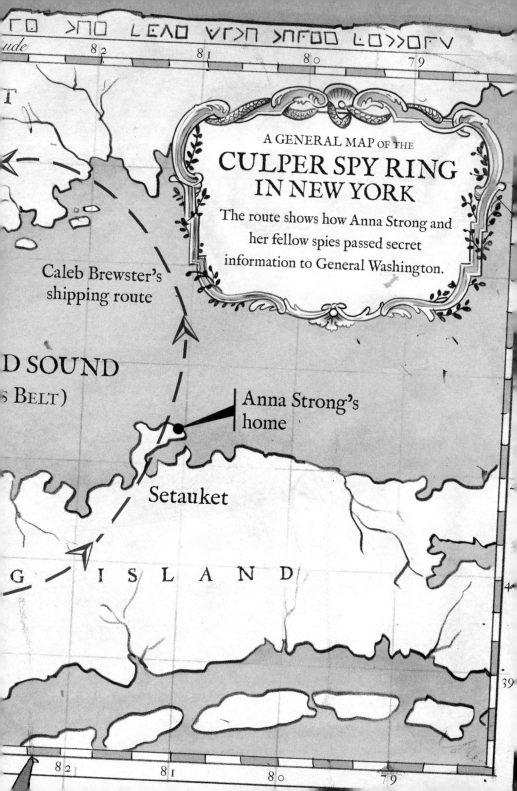

T

A GENERAL MAP OF THE

CULPER SPY RING IN NEW YORK

The route shows how Anna Strong and her fellow spies passed secret information to General Washington.

Caleb Brewster's shipping route

D SOUND
(BELT)

Anna Strong's home

Setauket

G   I S L A N D

Text by Enigma Alberti
Illustrations by Laura Terry

Library of Congress Cataloging-in-Publication Data is available.

ISBN 978-1-5235-0216-5

Design by Terri Ruffino

Workman books are available at special discounts when purchased in bulk for premiums and sales promotions as well as for fund-raising or educational use. Special editions or book excerpts can also be created to specification. For details, contact the Special Sales Director at the address below, or send an email to specialmarkets@workman.com.

Workman Publishing Co., Inc.
225 Varick Street
New York, NY 10014-4381

workman.com

Printed in China
First printing February 2019

10 9 8 7 6 5 4 3 2 1

This book tells a story of intrigue and danger.

There's also a mystery *in the book itself.*

At the end of the story, you'll find a letter from Anna.

Use the spycraft tools in this envelope to find clues and codes throughout the book . . .

and then decode Anna's letter and discover her secret mission!

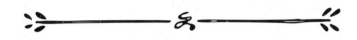

Anna Strong woke in the dark, her heart pounding. She was relieved to find herself in her own bed, beside her husband, Selah. Maybe the banging and shouts that had filled her dreams were nothing more than that—a bad dream.

Lord knew she'd had enough of those in the years since General George Washington lost the Battle of Brooklyn and retreated back to the mainland, leaving her beloved home of Long Island, New York, occupied by the invading army of hated British redcoats.

But as she took a deep breath, willing her heart to calm, a banging sounded at the front door. It wasn't just a dream.

The windows of the house shook with a tinny ring, as if someone had tapped them with something metal and sharp.

Bayonets? Anna wondered in the darkness.

"Open up in the name of His Majesty King George!" a voice shouted.

Beyond it, she could hear a host of other men's voices, some laughing, some swearing, some yelling threats.

The British liked to pretend they ran an orderly army, with their fine uniforms and their ramrod-straight lines of attack. But after years of British occupation, the American Patriots on Long Island knew better.

British soldiers treated the little coastal town of Setauket as if its only reason to exist was to raise livestock so

soldiers could **SWOOp in** and take WHATEVER they wanted, **whenever** they wanted.

Now and then, they left promissory notes as a pledge to pay later, but those weren't often honored. And the citizens who got those notes were the lucky ones. Most soldiers didn't even pretend to pay for what they took.

And it wasn't just livestock. Soldiers also used up crops and wood like locusts. One of Anna's neighbors had spent most of the past summer patching his pasture fences after the British tore them up for kindling.

But all of that was just an annoyance compared to the personal danger any Patriot now faced on the island. No man who had sided with the Americans for independence was safe from being roughed up by a passing gang of

British soldiers. No woman felt safe traveling the countryside alone.

And now the British had arrived on Anna's doorstep.

Selah sat up next to Anna in bed. Anna knew the noise had woken her children, too. She could hear one of the youngest whimpering with fear in the nearby children's room, and one of the others, slightly older, speaking in calming tones.

But at another volley of banging on the door, both children fell silent and the baby in the cradle at the foot of Anna's bed began to wail.

"What do they want?" she asked Selah.

"Stay here," he said. He threw aside the covers, picked up the musket that he kept beside the head of the bed, and slipped out of their bedroom.

Anna scooped up the baby and followed him. As soon as little Joseph felt his mother's heartbeat, his crying stopped and he began to nuzzle her neck, trying to find his way back to sleep.

Anna wished there was some magic that could calm her own fears so easily.

By the time she followed Selah down the hall to the great room of the house, he had already thrown open the front door to confront the British with nothing but his father's old musket.

A British officer swept THROUGH THE DOOR with three soldiers behind him.

More stood watch outside in the glistening January snow. Selah hadn't lit a lamp before going to the door, so Anna could only just make out their faces in the moonlight.

She could see the officer's face all too well, however. His features were so sharp and pale that they would have been hard to forget even if it weren't for the thin blue scar that crossed his cheek. But the cruelty in his eyes was burned into her mind even more.

"Selah Strong?" the officer said.

Another man might have hesitated before answering, but not Selah. He gave a curt nod, and without saying a word, he made his long-standing contempt for the abuses of authority by the British Empire perfectly clear.

"You're under arrest," the officer said, baring his teeth in a nasty grin.

"For what?" Anna blurted out, leaping forward.

The soldiers hadn't noticed Anna in the shadows. Now, at the sight of her, they all jumped. One man even started to raise his rifle.

"Don't you touch her," Selah barked.

The officer, who hadn't even flinched when Anna appeared, gestured to the soldier to lower his rifle. "Enough," he said calmly.

He nodded at Selah, and Anna watched as one of the soldiers stepped behind her husband and roughly bound his hands.

Anna's daughter Margaret, who had just turned ten, appeared in the hallway, blinking in the moonlight.

"Mama?" she said. At the sight of the soldiers, her eyes widened.

Keturah appeared behind Margaret. At seventeen, she was Anna's oldest child, and

it only took her
one glance
to UNDERSTAND
what was happening.

"Keturah," Anna said in a low voice, "take Margaret away."

Keturah nodded and pulled her little sister into the relative safety of the back rooms.

By the time Anna turned back to the door, Selah and the soldiers were gone. The only person left in the room with her and little Joseph was the officer.

"What is the charge?" Anna asked again. "Or has the British army given up following British law?"

The officer took a step forward, looking at Anna with strange fascination. She had the sickening feeling that he might touch her, but then he just sighed and turned to go.

"Correspondence with the enemy," he called over his shoulder.

The door banged shut behind him.

In the dark, Anna sank down into the old rocker where she had nursed each of her six children. She held little Joseph, less than a month old, to her chest.

Her heart pounded harder than ever, and it ached as she felt Selah moving away from her, carried off by the British into the night.

They thought Selah was a SPY, she realized.

How the British had gotten that idea, she didn't know. It was no secret that Selah was an American Patriot. He wasn't loyal to the British, but Anna and Selah had lived together safely through the years of the British occupation. Until now. Anna wondered if their Loyalist neighbors, who still considered themselves subjects of His Majesty King George III, had whispered something about Selah to a soldier.

Even as her mind raced and her chest tightened with worry for her husband, a smile crossed her lips.

The British might think that, by taking Selah, they had rooted out everyone in the Strong household who might cause them any trouble.

But as long as Anna was there, they hadn't.

Anna knocked on the door of her cousin's house. As she waited for an answer, she twisted the wedding ring on her finger.

She had just been to New York Harbor to visit Selah on the prison ship where he was being kept. The moment she stepped onto the ship, carrying bread and eggs and Long Island fruit to share with Selah, a deep fear began to gnaw at her heart.

She knew the smells of sea and ships and the smell of the men on board. That was just part of life on the coast in Setauket.

But the smell on this ship was something different, something rotten: the smell of death. The eyes of the prisoners were sunken, and their faces were taut from hunger.

She had hoped the conditions of Selah's prison might not be as bad as the rumors said. But they were worse— much worse.

When Selah was led out to her,

his hands and feet in IRON SHACKLES,

she saw the same look of starvation and mistreatment beginning to hollow out his features.

"I'm fine, Nancy," he assured her, using her nickname as he gratefully bit into an apple she had brought. But, watching his gaunt face, she knew

if he stayed much longer on that FETID SHIP, he would die.

And he wouldn't be the first one. Setauket's Reverend Benjamin Tallmadge was still mourning the death of one of his sons, William, who had been captured shortly after the Battle of Brooklyn and died on a prison ship. The reverend's other son, Benjamin Junior, was supposedly one of Washington's most trusted aides. Even so, he hadn't been able to save his brother's life once William fell into British hands.

Anna pushed the thought of the prison ship out of her mind. She shifted from one foot to the other, wondering if she should knock on her cousin's door again. Anna knew this house. She had been there many times as a child, but since the war began, family relations had cooled. This side of Anna's family had Loyalist leanings. Unlike Anna and Selah, they still considered themselves subjects of the king. In British-occupied New York, they held considerable influence.

Which was why Anna had come here, straight from the prison ship.

Just as she was about to knock again, the door swung open.

Anna's wealthy cousin wasn't thrilled to see her. He looked even less thrilled when, only moments after he served her a very fine cup of tea, she broached the subject of Selah's arrest.

"My goodness," he said. "What were the charges?"

Anna had to swallow her anger as she responded, "Correspondence with the enemy."

"Is there any truth to it?" her cousin asked.

Anna shook her head. "You know Selah's opinions," she said. "But so does everybody else on Long Island, including the Loyalists and the redcoats."

Long Island was a hotbed of Loyalists. They advertised their loyalty to the crown by serving in garrisons and wearing green military coats. In fact, there were more Loyalists with green coats on the island than there were British soldiers with red coats.

"So Selah couldn't be a spy," Anna said. "He was watched everywhere he went."

"Are you **sure** about that?" her cousin asked, raising his eyebrows.

Anna set aside her tea and leaned forward, tears springing to her eyes. "He'll die if he stays on that ship," she said. "Whatever he did, do you think he deserves that?"

Her cousin shifted uncomfortably in his seat.

"Please," Anna pleaded. "Please. You were at our wedding."

A smile played on his lips. "I remember," he said. "Some of the younger cousins tried to dunk Selah in a nearby lake."

Anna realized that her cousin was fondly thinking back to better times. That was a good sign. "As I recall, you were one of those younger cousins," she said.

He sighed. "This whole WAR is a shame.

"I don't know how the colonies got it into their heads that they could stand against the greatest navy in the world and the best-trained soldiers."

A few tart words about the way the British had misused their power rose to Anna's lips. The Loyalists still seemed to think that the war was about a silly matter of taxes. But in the years since the war began, it had gone far beyond that. The Patriots weren't just fighting for fewer taxes. They were fighting for true independence.

But Anna held her tongue, doing her best to treat her cousin with openness and warmth so he would agree to help her husband.

Finally, he leaned back in his seat.

"I can't make you any promises," he said. "But I'LL DO WHAT I CAN."

Anna leapt out of her seat to hug him. "Thank you," she said. "I'll never be able to repay you."

He disentangled himself from her, bemused. But she could see he liked playing the role of benefactor.

"And don't be a stranger," he told her. "We shouldn't let a little matter like this war break up the family."

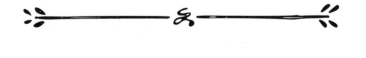

The house had been eerily silent ever since Selah had been released from the prison ship. Even though her cousin had managed to secure Selah's release, it was too dangerous for Selah to come back to Setauket while the British still controlled it. So he had gone to join Patriot relatives in Connecticut, which was held by General Washington and his troops.

But Anna and Selah had decided that Anna would stay on their property to keep it from being plundered by the British. They had seen what had happened to the homes of friends who had abandoned their property as they fled, and it wasn't pretty.

To protect the children from any further harassment by the British, Anna had taken them to Connecticut to join Selah—all save baby Joseph, who was too young to be away from her.

So she and baby Joseph had been LIVING BY THEMSELVES in the big house.

It seemed so quiet now that it wasn't full of family—quiet enough that Anna could hear the timid knock on the door.

Anna's mind raced, wondering who could be knocking. Was it the bandits who now roamed the uprooted communities of Long Island? Would they sneakily knock to see if anyone was there, before breaking into the house?

And if they were bandits, what could Anna do to stop them?

Joseph was asleep in her bedroom, so her hands were free to grasp Selah's musket, which the British hadn't bothered to confiscate when they arrested him. They probably didn't imagine that she would ever use it herself.

Silently, she raised it to her shoulder and trained it on the door.

"Who's there?" she called.

The answering voice was almost as QUIET as the knock, but it was so familiar that she RECOGNIZED IT INSTANTLY.

It was her neighbor Abraham Woodhull. Anna and Selah had known him for years.

"Anna," he whispered. "Let me in. I need your help."

Anna studied Abraham's face, thinking about how much times had changed.

Abraham had been just a boy when Anna was a young woman. She remembered him letting a frog loose once during church when Ben Tallmadge's father, the reverend, was preaching. Anna had never been able to take Abraham seriously when he came over from his neighboring farm on some little item of business, like returning a wandering pig or asking for seeds so he could finish planting the kitchen garden.

But now Abraham was clearly all grown up. He picked at the sleeves of his coat nervously as he spoke to Anna, but his eyes were clear and the story he told was enough to make anyone nervous.

"It's about Ben," he told her as he shuffled into the house. Anna's heart sank, wondering how Reverend Tallmadge would bear it if something happened to his other son. She turned to the table by the door, ready to strike a match and light a lamp, but Abraham shook his head.

"No one can know I'm here."

They sat down together in the chairs by the fire, where Selah used to read to her during the long winter nights. "Don't worry, Ben is fine," Abraham assured her. "In fact, I saw Ben just a few days ago.

General Washington needs INTELLIGENCE

and he's put Ben in charge of it, so Ben came to talk to me."

"To you?" Anna said.

As soon as she said it, she worried Abraham could hear the surprise in her voice.

But Abraham shook his head ruefully to show that he was just as surprised as Anna.

"Washington has tried to send spies across enemy lines before," he said. "But they're too easy to identify. You heard about Nathan Hale."

Anna nodded. The story had struck close to home. Nathan Hale had been a good friend of Ben's when they were both students at Yale. Nathan had been barely twenty-one when he volunteered for a secret mission. He had tried to gather evidence while posing as a teacher in British-occupied territory, but he wasn't from the area.

Nathan was identified as a spy within days and executed almost immediately after he was captured.

...ded with the odious names of Rebels and Traitors, yet we fight for Liberty. I only regret that I hAve but 1 life to lose for my country.

Your loving son,

Nathan Hale

"Ben says he needs people who can gather information for him without leaving their daily business," Abraham went on.

"People he knows he can TRUST."

He gazed out the window. The moonlight glimmered in the water of Long Island Sound. "Look at where we are," he said. "The entire British navy is out on those waters, and Washington's Continental Army is just across the sound." Anna nodded.

"You and I are in the perfect position to help Ben," Abraham went on. "My trading takes me into New York City regularly, the heart of what's now enemy territory. And you learn about the British army simply by being one of the unfortunate residents of Long Island under their occupation."

As Anna realized she may have a role to play, she felt breathless at the opportunities.

"What can I do to help?" she asked.

Abraham looked at her gratefully. "Your house is at a high point on the coast," he said.

"It can be seen from the WHOLE SOUND. You know Caleb Brewster?"

Anna nodded. Caleb was a rough-and-tumble captain of various small ships. He was rumored to be running the smuggling trade between New York City and Long Island. He made a living taking fresh Long Island food to the city and returning with fine goods that were almost impossible to get on Long Island now: tea, thread, and sugar. It was illegal, of course, but most people were grateful for Caleb's services. Plus, he was a longtime Setauket resident, known locally to be a good and brave man.

"He can take messages across the sound to American-occupied territory where Ben can get them," said Abraham.

"I sign the messages 'SAMUEL CULPER, SR.' so only Ben will know who they're from.

But I need someone to signal Caleb when I have a message for him to deliver. A signal the British will never guess."

"My laundry!" Anna said instantly. "I hang it up on the top of the hill to catch the sea breeze. It might as well be a string of flags."

"That might work . . ." Abraham said.

"Tell him to look for a black petticoat," Anna said decisively. "If he sees that, he'll know you have a message for him."

Abraham nodded. "The other challenge is that I don't want to meet him in the same place each time," he said. "If I'm ever followed, they'll know where to find us the next time."

"There are half a dozen coves in Setauket," Anna said. "And I have half a dozen handkerchiefs. Tell him to count the handkerchiefs to figure out which cove to go to."

For the first time since he had stepped into her house, Abraham smiled.

"I think . . . I think that will work."

"Of course it will," Anna said.

But Abraham's smile suddenly disappeared.

"Is there something else?" Anna asked.

"I hate to ask this," he said. "I don't have any right."

Anna sighed impatiently. "The British army locked my husband up on a ship to die," she said. "If I can do something more than hang a petticoat on a line, I want to know about it."

"I can't stop thinking about Nathan Hale," Abraham said, looking down as if he was ashamed of himself. "I'm going to be doing the same thing he did, gathering information in enemy territory. But I don't want to die the way he did."

Anna nodded.

"I've been watching the redcoats at the checkpoints," Abraham said. "They aren't kind to a man traveling alone. But if he's with his wife and child . . ." He looked up.

"And I know you have family of your own in NEW YORK CITY."

"I'll come with you," Anna said.

Abraham's smile returned.

"**W**here are you going?" the redcoat growled. Abraham shifted nervously beside Anna on the seat of the wagon. "New York City," he answered.

Anna bit her tongue to hold back her annoyance with him. The redcoat hadn't been paying any attention to them before Abraham started fidgeting.

If Abraham had just STAYED CALM, they would be through the ROADBLOCK by now.

They had passed through the last two on their way to the city without incident.

But now the redcoat was peering at Abraham, suspicion in his eyes.

"What for?" the redcoat demanded.

"Business," Abraham answered uneasily.

"What kind of business?"

"We've got a pile of goods in the back to feed your army and your army's horses," Anna said tartly. "And I'm coming along because he can't be trusted to buy the fancy goods I want from the city. The last time I sent him to buy me a yard of lace, he brought back a potato sack."

The redcoat's expression shifted from suspicion of Abraham to sympathy for him. Abraham certainly seemed to have a sharp-tongued wife!

"You got any apples in there?" the redcoat asked. Abraham glanced at Anna.

She reached back, pulled aside the corner of the tarp over their load, and produced three crisp apples.

"Best of the season," she said proudly, handing them over. "You won't find any sweeter."

The redcoat GRINNED as he took a bite of one and pocketed the others.

Then he waved his hand for the other soldiers to move the rough sawhorses that blocked the road and rapped on the side of the wagon.

"Drive on," he said.

To Purchase—

To General Washington

Lace

Along with the letter I am sending a new Method

Sewing pins

for carrying on Correspondence in future

Linen for Tablecloths

From now on no one can read our Letters

Thread

who does not have one of these as well

two pairs cotton Stockings

Your most obedient humble servant

Candles

Samuel Culper Jr.

no Potato Sacks

Anna had already heard about the huge fire that reduced the lower end of New York to cinders. To see it in person, however, was another thing entirely.

Blocks of the city—houses, shops, even docks—had all been burned to ashes. And so far, nothing had been built to replace them except for an ugly collection of shanties and tents filled with criminals and the destitute.

"The fire destroyed so much more than I would have believed," Anna murmured. "Who could have set it?"

"Nobody knows," Abraham told her. "The Americans say the British started it, and the British say the Americans started it. But maybe it was started by a couple of soldiers' wives just trying to keep warm."

He pulled the team of horses up outside a mercantile house.

"We have business here?" Anna asked.

Abraham, who had relaxed considerably since they passed the last guard post on the way to the city, winked.

"I've got a new friend here—Robert Townsend," he said. "He's on our side, but he masquerades as a Tory trader. He even owns part of one of the most popular Loyalist coffee-houses in Manhattan."

Anna raised her eyebrows.

"That sounds like a good place
to hear all the latest
LOYALIST GOSSIP," she said.

Abraham's eyes glinted. "That's right," he said. "Just the kind of spot for good Loyalists like us."

W hen Anna returned from trips to the city with Abraham, her house felt empty and quiet. Every time she heard hooves on the road, she hoped it might be Selah, coming home.

She knew it wasn't safe for him yet on Long Island, and that it would not be safe until the war was won. But her heart never stopped waiting for him.

One day, as she hung her black petticoat on the line, a visitor approached. Anna froze. It was the officer who had come in the night to take Selah away.

He trotted up and gave her a courtly grin.

"Mrs. Strong," he said. "Good afternoon."

"Can I help you with something?" Anna asked curtly.

The officer shook his head. "Oh no, oh no," he said. "I just think it's good for an army to stay friendly with its neighbors. Don't you agree?"

Anna didn't answer. She just bent over to pick another handkerchief out of her washing basket.

Abraham had slipped over the night before to let her know what signal to give Caleb today, and it gave Anna pleasure

to put out THE CODE right under the officer's nose.

But as she worked, the officer's eyes narrowed. "So many handkerchiefs," he said. "I trust you've been feeling well?"

Anna felt a chill run down her spine, but that didn't stop her from picking up another handkerchief and hanging it out.

"And what an interesting color for a petticoat," the officer went on. "I thought I saw you hang up one like it just last week."

"Is this what passes for friendly in the British army these days? Spying on your neighbor's laundry line?"

"And such a strange combination of wash," the officer went on. "Petticoats and handkerchiefs."

"When was the last time you did a woman's wash?" Anna asked.

The officer laughed, but his eyes remained cold and serious.

He looked at Anna for another long moment, unsmiling, before he rode off again.

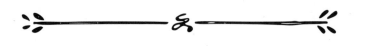

The next time Anna saw Abraham, he was clearly anxious.

"Every message I get from Ben says the same thing," Abraham replied, wiping his feverish brow. "General Washington says we're sending the most useful intelligence. But he has to get it faster in order to act on it."

Anna sat back in her chair, frustrated. She and Abraham still made occasional trips to New York City together, but to speed up the flow of information, they had recruited Austin Roe, the owner of a local Setauket tavern. Roe began visiting New York and meeting with their new friend Robert Townsend, who was secretly spying on the British for General Washington. Roe had a good excuse for traveling often to the city—buying supplies for the tavern.

And, Anna suspected, the British soldiers liked taking bribes of Roe's liquor more than they enjoyed Abraham's apples.

Anna supplied Roe with

PLENTY OF

TRAVEL EXCUSES

of her own.

She sent orders with him for yards and yards of tablecloths, candles, tea, and any fancy goods she could think of—and afford—with written instructions that they should be

perfect	480	poverty	514
pilot	481	power	515
prudent	482	prosperous	516
publish	483	punishment	517
purchase	484	preferment	518
purpose	485	production	519
people	486	pursuant	520
pleasure	487	pensioner	521
produce	488	Parliament	522
prison	489	persecution	523
progress	490	practicable	524
promise	491	profitable	525
proper	492	particular	526
prosper	493	petition	527
prospect	494	profession	528
punish	495	proclaim	529
partake	496	provision	530
perform	497	protection	531
permit	498	*2*	
pervert	499	quick	532
prepare	500	question	533
prevail	501	quantity	534

robber	547	rebellion	581
render	548	reduction	582
ruin	549	remarkable	583
ruler	550	reinforce	584
rapid	551	refugee	585
reader	552	*S*	
rebel	553	sail	586
rigor	664	see	587
river	555	sea	588
receipt	556	scheme	589
reft.	557	set	590
regain	558	send	591
rejoice	559	ship	592
relate	560	safe	593
request	561	same	594
relax	562	sky	595
redoubt	563	secret	596
relay	564	seldom	597
remit	565	sentence	598
reprieve	566	servant	599
repulse	567	signal	600

purchased in the greatest haste. This way, Roe had a good reason to be just about anywhere in the city his work might lead him.

But the information still wasn't being delivered fast enough for General Washington.

Anna had an idea. "What if we found a messenger in New York City to take the information to Washington, instead of bringing it back to Long Island first?"

Abraham shook his head. "We can't involve any outsiders," he said. "Almost everyone in this spy ring has known each other since we were babies. That's the only reason we're still alive."

"Not Townsend," Anna said.

"That's true," Abraham said. "But the more strangers we add, the more chance of—"

He was interrupted when Anna's front door BANGED OPEN, revealing Austin Roe.

Behind Austin, a horse pranced breathlessly in the yard, hastily tied to Anna's hitching post. Austin himself was almost as winded as his animal.

"Woodhull," he said, barely bothering to look at Anna. "I heard you were here. I've got news. News we've got to get to General Washington. The French fleet has arrived in Newport, Rhode Island, to fight for the Americans, but General Clinton is about to send the British fleet to meet them. If he does, the French will be destroyed."

45

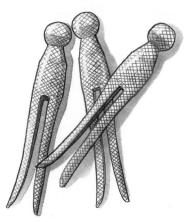

Anna shared a quick look with Abraham. The French joining the war could mean the fledgling American nation had a shot at winning—and Selah might have the chance to return home safely. But if the British crushed the first bit of help the French sent, there was no guarantee the French would ever send more aid.

"If you'll excuse me," Anna said, slipping toward the door. "I have some laundry I need to hang."

Roe didn't know Anna was part of the spy ring, which was fine with her. As Abraham had pointed out, the less each of them knew, the safer they all were.

At the door, she glanced at Abraham again for a sign.

He raised two fingers as he began to jot down the details that Roe was sharing about Clinton's plans.

So Abraham wants to meet Caleb at the second cove, Anna thought. A moment later, she was outside, hanging two handkerchiefs on her line.

C aleb answered the signal and Abraham snuck down to Setauket's second cove to give Caleb the precious information that might save the French fleet.

But Anna didn't know if anyone saw Abraham coming and going.

Or what happened to Caleb after he sailed out of the cove.

Or what the redcoats would do if they discovered there were spies in their midst.

A few days later, as Anna tended her garden, she saw a red-coated figure crest the low hill near her house. A shiver ran down her spine.

Behind the first redcoat, three more appeared, and behind them, another three, and another, until most of an entire company of soldiers was flowing down the narrow road to her home.

Had they sent out all these soldiers JUST TO CAPTURE HER?

Anna was torn between disbelief, pride, and a deep desire to run.

But she knew they had seen her, and the British had taken every good horse on the farm, except for dear old Franklin, who was so old he could barely pull a plow. Whether on foot or on Franklin, Anna could never outrun the soldiers' mounts, even though she knew the country-side better than any of them.

So she stood her ground.

In fact, she kept tending the garden, pulling out the first carrots of the summer and gathering them into her wooden basket.

To her surprise, when the soldiers got near, they broke out of formation and scattered past her as if she didn't exist. They rode up to her house like they owned it. As she watched, one of them dismounted, tossed the reins of his horse to another soldier, and walked through her front door.

Anna scooped up her baby, who was napping in a carrying crib between the garden rows, and ran toward the house.

"STOP!" she shouted. "What are you doing?"

By the time she burst into her living room, the officer had taken off his red coat and thrown it over one of the dining room chairs. He was helping himself to a cup of water from Anna's favorite pewter pitcher.

She had never liked his odd, dead-eyed smile, but this time there was no trace of it, and she discovered she liked his face without a smile even less.

"Mrs. Strong," the officer said coldly, taking a seat at Anna's table.

Anna resisted the urge to give him a good tongue-lashing and throw him out of her house. Too many other women on Long Island had already learned that the British army didn't have much respect for them. She didn't want to give him any excuse for violence.

So instead, she forced herself to smile.

"What brings you here?" she asked.

"I'm **afraid** your home is needed by the BRITISH ARMY," the officer said.

"As a loyal citizen of the crown, I'm sure you'll be glad to do anything you can for the king at this challenging moment."

Anna's mind raced, barely able to take in what was happening.

"Challenging?" she repeated.

The officer looked at her with sharp impatience. "Don't say that as if you don't know," he said.

Anna shifted the sleepy baby from one arm to the other.

"The battle with the French in Rhode Island," the officer said. "Or rather, the one that didn't happen."

Anna's heart leapt, but she fought to keep her face expressionless. Had their tiny spy ring been successful? Had Anna and Abraham helped save the French fleet by getting information about General Clinton's planned attack to Caleb?

"The French were in Rhode Island?" Anna asked, trying her best to sound innocent.

"And General Clinton was on his way there," the officer said. "Until he received word that Washington was planning an attack further south. Clinton lit signal fires all the way down the coast, calling the British fleet back before they could attack. I'm surprised you couldn't see them from your land."

"It's fifteen miles across the sound to Connecticut," Anna told him. Inside, her heart was singing in victory.

The officer watched her closely. "It turned out," he said,

"the **report** of Washington's attack to the south was a **FALSE ALARM**.

By the time Clinton found out that it was a ruse, the French fleet had been warned he was nearby. Now that the French have arrived safely, they will be able to join the war."

He stood up and set the tin cup on her table.

"In these dark days for the British army," he said, "we find ourselves in need of comfort. I, for one, was not looking forward to spending another winter in a run-down farmhouse. And your home is so large for just you and the one child."

"My home?" Anna repeated.

"I'll be moving in here,"
THE OFFICER INFORMED HER.

"Along with a few other luminaries of our force here on Long Island."

Anna stared at him, holding the baby close.

"I believe I've seen a little cottage at the foot of the property?" the officer said. "Down near the water."

"The watchman's cottage?" Anna asked.

The officer nodded. "That should be big enough for just the two of you," he said. "Shouldn't it?"

As Anna continued to stand there, staring at him, he waved his hand grandly toward the back of the house, where the children's toys and treasures were kept, along with the linens she'd washed and the clothes she'd made. They would all be at the mercy of the officers who were about to take up residence here.

"Take your time packing," the officer said. "I'm in no hurry, since I have no plans to leave."

Anna had never been someone who loved to gossip. She loved to listen to the crashing ocean waves in Setauket. She loved to listen to the hustle and bustle of the streets of New York. But she'd never seen much point in spending hours listening to people talk about what other people wore or said. Whenever she came to the city, however, she couldn't avoid gossip.

Her cousin was influential with the British, so she often claimed to be on her way to visit him when she and Abraham had trouble getting past roadblocks on the way to the city. And if she said she was visiting her cousin, she knew she *had* to make the visit so she didn't raise any suspicion.

And so she spent long hours in drawing rooms and at fancy balls, smiling through gritted teeth as her cousin's daughters and their friends danced with British officers and traded gossip.

Looking at them all, you would think the war was one big PARTY, with not a single life at stake, let alone the FREEDOM OF A WHOLE NATION.

"That's not what Peggy told me," Tansy was saying to her friend Becca.

The two girls sat next to Anna on a cushioned bench in the drawing room where Anna's cousin was throwing a small dance.

Anna thought wistfully of baby Joseph, napping upstairs. Sometimes the baby would start squalling just at the moment Anna's own nerves were about to break from frustration, giving her the perfect excuse to step away.

But right now she had no such luck. She would be sitting there, she feared, until the musicians played their last notes.

"Oh, that Peggy," Becca said dismissively. "She's so dramatic. I heard she had a fit once when there was too much sugar in the punch."

Tansy laughed. "Well, I heard she said this whole war will be over by Christmas. And she should know."

Anna was confused. Christmas was only a few short months away, and the war was at a perfect stalemate. The Americans had succeeded in driving the British out of Philadelphia, but Charleston had fallen into British hands. As far as Anna knew, the war wasn't going to be over anytime soon.

"And how would Peggy know?" Anna asked.

Tansy's eyes lit up, surprised to have finally gained Anna's attention. "Well, it's Peggy Shippen," she said. "General Arnold's new wife."

That PIQUED Anna's interest.

Maybe gossip COULD BE INTERESTING after all.

Anna had heard that General Benedict Arnold was the greatest hero of the war. In the early days of the fighting, he had singlehandedly run off a small fleet of British ships on

the waterways north of New York. That act had prevented the redcoats from splitting New England from New York and winning the war right then and there.

Arnold had also turned the tide of the Battle of Saratoga, where he led a force of soldiers into the thick of the fiercest fighting and received a terrible leg wound in the process.

He may have been a hero, but Arnold was also known to be moody and boastful. It didn't surprise Anna that he was trumpeting claims about victory that no officer in his right mind would make.

"And how, pray tell, does General Arnold think the Americans will win this war by Christmas?" Anna asked.

"Oh," Tansy said, "not the Americans."

Anna's brow knit in confusion. "General Arnold doesn't think the Americans can win this war?" she said.

"Nobody thinks that the Americans can win this war," Becca said.

Tansy looked at Anna with pity. "The British," she clarified.

"Peggy Shippen says the
BRITISH
will win the war
by Christmas.

She can't wait for it to be over. None of us can. This war has been such a *bore*."

"General Arnold's wife is itching for the British to win this war?" Anna asked. "And General Arnold allows her to go around saying so?"

"He's the one who told her," Tansy said. "She said he was planning to make sure the British won."

The HAIR stood up on the back of Anna's neck.

The story was so improbable she could barely believe it. General Arnold couldn't be a traitor—he was a Patriot hero. But something told her that Tansy would never have made this up on her own.

Could it possibly be true?

"How does he intend to do that?" Anna asked, as if she was only interested in trading gossip.

Tansy shrugged. "How would I know?" she said. "But Peggy swore Arnold has a plan."

Abraham flicked the reins, urging his horses to leave the British checkpoint where he and Anna had just been stopped on their way out of New York City.

Now that the open fields stretched out around them, they could finally speak freely about General Arnold.

"I can hardly believe it," Abraham said. "I don't understand how a man could turn traitor like that. Just about everything else in this war makes sense to me, even if I don't like it. But General Arnold has been wounded twice fighting for the American cause. He's one of Washington's most trusted men."

Anna smiled wryly. "So you *do* believe me?"

Abraham sighed. "After you told me what you heard at the party, I had Townsend make some inquiries among the British officers."

"And?" Anna asked.

Abraham shifted on the wagon's seat. "I wish I knew more," he said. "Townsend couldn't get many details. But when he mentioned the idea of General Arnold working with the British, one of his contacts asked him how he'd found out about it."

Anna's heart dropped. Until now, she had half hoped that the news Tansy had given her was just made-up gossip.

"But they don't know what General Arnold plans to do?" she asked.

Abraham shook his head. "I'm not sure it matters," he said. "Arnold is in control of the fort at West Point now. It commands the whole Hudson River. We only hold that fort because Arnold held back a British fleet at the beginning of the war."

"That means if we LOSE West Point," said Anna, "we would LOSE the whole river."

Abraham nodded grimly. "Not just the river," he said. "That river connects the Continental Army to New England in the north. The American forts north of New York are the only thing keeping the entire British navy from sailing up the Hudson to conquer New England. So if the British take West Point . . ."

"... then the war is over," Anna said quietly.

"If Arnold's not loyal, the whole war hangs in the balance," said Abraham.

Anna looked impatiently down the road.

"Can these horses go any *FASTER?"* she asked.

"We'll be home in time for you to hang out the signal for Caleb before nightfall," Abraham said. "I'll meet with him tonight. I just hope we can get the word about Arnold to Washington in time."

Anna knew by the three light knocks that it was Caleb at the door.

At Abraham's request, she had hung an extra handkerchief on the line that afternoon to signal a meeting at the watchman's cottage where she had been staying with the baby ever since the British took over the big house.

Abraham was running late. Anna knew he agonized over the reports he sent to Ben Tallmadge because he didn't think he was good at writing. Maybe he was taking his time to write this one.

Or maybe he was worried for his SAFETY.

It would be easy for Caleb to come and go. The little house at the foot of Anna's property was conveniently close to the water. Caleb would be able to slip right back to his boat after collecting Abraham's message.

But it wasn't so simple for Abraham. On any other day, he could take his time going to a cove to meet Caleb, to be sure that he wasn't followed on the way. But with this emergency meeting happening at night, Anna worried Abraham might encounter a British patrol on the way. It would be hard for him to explain why he was skulking down by the ocean in the dark.

At Caleb's knock, Anna quickly darkened the lamp she had been reading by so the light wouldn't alert the nearby British when she opened the door.

She drew the door open and Caleb nodded in greeting—then both of them froze.

Hoofbeats

POUNDED TOWARD THEM
through the darkness,
coming down from the big house.

"Has Abraham gone mad?" Caleb hissed. "Does he want to wake the king's whole army?"

Anna shook her head. "That's not Abraham," she said. "He'd never ride here from his place. It would draw too much attention."

A horseman emerged from the surrounding dark and halted a short distance from the cottage. The horse pranced a few steps as the rider looked around.

Since Anna had put the lamp out, the horseman could not see her and Caleb at the door. But Anna thought she saw a flash of red coat in the moonlight.

Silently, Caleb gestured for her to retreat into the cottage.

Anna slipped behind the door, but didn't close it. She kept peering out, her heart pounding, while Caleb vanished behind a nearby hedge.

The rider walked his mount a few steps closer to the cottage.

Anna's chest tightened. Had this rider been here before? How many other British soldiers had lurked outside her door, unbeknownst to her?

The rider was so close now that Anna could see his face, greedy and pale in the moonlight. He was squinting through the darkness, trying to see into her windows.

Just as he began to dismount from his horse, Caleb burst from the hedge.

One instant the man was sitting atop his horse. The next he was a heap on the ground, his horse stepping skittishly away.

Anna heard a SERIES OF THUMPS as Caleb struck the man, blow after blow.

Anna began to fear for the soldier's life. The same thought seemed to occur to Caleb. Finally, he held back his fist.

"Your wallet," Caleb growled.

"We ain't been paid in a month," said the soldier.

Anna heard the sound of another blow and rustling as Caleb sifted through the man's pockets.

"That's my last tobacco," the soldier complained.

Caleb stashed it in his own pocket. Then he dragged the man to his feet. "Go on," he snarled. "Get out of here."

The soldier reeled, glaring at him. But when Caleb raised his fist, the soldier flinched. He whistled for his horse, clambered up on it, and galloped back into the dark.

Caleb lumbered to Anna's door, breathless.

"I thought you were going to kill him," Anna whispered.

"I thought about it," Caleb told her. "But I think he got the message. He won't be back."

Behind Caleb, somebody else was suddenly approaching.

Caleb whirled around, and he and Anna caught their breath.

But this time, it was Abraham, bearing a message for General Washington.

"**D**id you hear about General Arnold?"

The woman who was speaking stood behind Anna in the general store. It was all Anna could do not to whirl around at the question.

But she held still, keeping her face blank as she pretended to inspect a piece of lace. The woman, who Anna recognized as a local Loyalist, kept talking to her friend.

"These Patriots!" she said. "Even their own generals don't think they can win this war. My husband just got back from New York with the news. It seems General Arnold came over to our side months ago. The British planned the whole thing so this ridiculous war could finally be over. But a couple of ruffians discovered General Arnold's plot. Poor luck!"

The woman accepted her change from the clerk.

"I don't know how they ever FOUND HIM OUT," she said.

"Everyone has always said General Arnold is such a smart man."

As the woman left the store, Anna wondered if the good news was true.

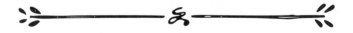

It took weeks to gather EACH VERSION OF THE STORY from the papers and gossip.

In the end, General Arnold's betrayal was even worse than Anna had thought. Tansy had been right: Arnold had hatched a plan with the British.

He had fought bravely on the side of the Americans for years. On his own initiative, just after the first battles of the war at Lexington and Concord, he had taken over Fort Ticonderoga along with Ethan Allen. While Allen and his men were helping themselves to the fort's liquor stores, Arnold took fifty men up to Lake Champlain, where he captured another fort and the largest British ship on the lake, which he renamed the *Enterprise*.

But as the war progressed, Arnold had watched bad behavior among the American soldiers go unchecked. He had watched men with less experience get more recognition than he had gotten or take credit for his victories.

Although he was one of the country's most formidable generals, he was denied a promotion by the Continental Congress.

Arnold wasn't the only general upset by how the war was being managed. The Continental Congress had also been driving General Washington to distraction. Worried that a strong military commander could turn into a dictator, Congress never gave him enough money and insisted on interfering with the tiniest details of military life.

But General Arnold wasn't just frustrated. After receiving two terrible wounds in the service of a country he didn't believe valued him, he became bitter. At that point, it was easy for his Loyalist wife, Peggy, to convince him to turn his bitterness into treason.

She had argued it wasn't treason at all. Almost every man in the Continental Army had once been loyal to the king. From Peggy's point of view, it was the Americans who were the traitors.

And not only that, it looked very much like they were going to lose the war. So why shouldn't Arnold return to his proper loyalties, and to the winning side?

When it was put that way, it sounded smart, even honorable.

But what Arnold actually plotted was HORRIBLE.

Arnold had been in correspondence with John André, the young head of British intelligence. Together, they hatched a plan for Arnold to surrender West Point to the British and make the American soldiers under his command British prisoners.

Thousands of American prisoners of war had already died on ships like the one where Anna's husband had been imprisoned. The same fate would probably have befallen Arnold's men.

Not only that, Arnold planned to do it on a day when General Washington was scheduled to visit West Point. Arnold wasn't just surrendering the fort. He was betraying a person who had trusted him for years, the same person who had given him the command at West Point.

It was a solid plan, and it probably would have worked if Arnold hadn't been caught just in time.

John André had ventured across the Hudson to meet with Arnold and lay the final plans. But on his way back, André was stopped on the road by a few American guards. They searched him and found documents exposing the West Point plot hidden in his boots. They didn't know that Arnold was involved—but when Ben Tallmadge heard the news, he knew that treason was afoot. The Americans discovered that the documents in André's boots were from Arnold himself, and the traitor was exposed!

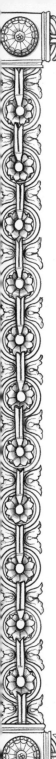

André was charged and hanged as a spy, while Arnold fled down the river to the protection of the British and into eternal disgrace in the eyes of Americans.

Back on Long Island, still under the yoke of British occupation, Anna and her friends had the silent satisfaction of knowing Tallmadge recognized the signs of treason

because of the SECRET INFORMATION they had sent him.

The work Anna, Abraham, and their friends did and the risks they took had saved the Continental Army from certain and immediate defeat.

But at first, it also hurt the Patriots.

John André had been beloved, a favorite of the British general Clinton, who was furious about André's execution. He made conditions terrible for the Americans under British occupation. It became so difficult to travel that for months Anna didn't hang a single signal from her clothesline. Bandits roamed the roads along with British soldiers, and from the way both behaved, it was hard to tell the difference between them. In the winter, food was scarce on Long Island.

But despite the odds, the Continental Army BATTLED ON.

Almost exactly a year after General Arnold's treason was discovered, the French navy fought the British fleet to a draw on the Chesapeake, which kept the British army trapped by Washington's forces in Yorktown, Virginia. A month later, the British at Yorktown—General Cornwallis and his entire army—surrendered to the Continental Army and their French allies.

On the day Anna heard the wonderful news, the seaside snow was beginning to melt under the spring sun and there was strange activity up at the big house.

Usually, the officers garrisoned there took their time getting up in the morning. This far from actual battles, they were just a standing army.

But this morning, there was a BUSTLE OF ACTIVITY in Anna's yard.

Curious, Anna took the hand of little Joseph, who was toddling now, and walked up the hill.

Half of the men were grinning. Half of them were cursing. Anna didn't know what to make of it.

The officer with the scar on his face was sitting on her porch with his feet up on the rail that Selah had built. He caught sight of her and waved her up.

Anna came to a stop at the foot of the stairs.

"Mrs. Strong," he said, not bothering to rise. "I am delighted to inform you that you'll be able to take occupation of your fine home again soon."

Anna's ears perked up. Were the British mustering all their forces for one great, decisive battle? Would she have more news to share, another secret meeting to arrange between Abraham and Caleb?

She glanced around the yard. The men might be upset, but they were healthy, strong, in good shape, and well fed. They had not been tired out by years of war. Could the American army stand against the full force of soldiers like these?

"You're moving off the island?" she asked.

"Even better than that," the officer said. "We're leaving this pestilent backwater for England. We're going home."

Anna's eyebrows knit in confusion, which made the officer smile.

"Parliament's voted," he said. "They don't think your land is worth fighting for."

"THE WAR IS OVER?" Anna asked, disbelief mingling with joy in her chest.

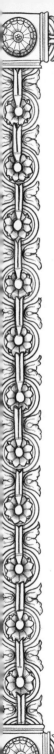

"Your independence has been recognized," the officer said. He looked around her yard, trampled into mud by the boots of his men, and his lip curled. "Such as it is."

Then he gave her a sly look. "I'm sure that comes as a disappointment to you," he said. "Since you were always so loyal to the crown."

Without answering, Anna scooped up Joseph and walked away, taking the familiar path between her farm and Abraham's.

When she reached his yard, she ran the last few steps, Joseph laughing in her arms.

She banged on the door excitedly until Abraham answered.

When he came to the door, he looked worn and weary from the long winter, but she knew that what she had to say would lift his mood.

"Abraham," she said breathlessly.

"I've got news. WONDERFUL news. You'll hardly BELIEVE what I just heard..."

Can you decipher Anna's letter to Caleb Brewster?

725,

682   e l i   229   431   380   390   282

439   634   506   625   347   682   348.

ns   meuv   ijjqlv   yeu   vq   himcxil   vbi

lixcuih   xilucqp   qj   vbi   gwmril   gqhi

vq   qpi   qj   vbi   uivewoiv   gqxiu.

gep   sqw   aiv   vbcu   gqrs   uejims   vq

aipilem   yeubcpavqp?

fi   ueji,

eppe

Historical Note

The identities of many members of the Culper Spy Ring were a mystery until 1929, when a sharp-eyed historian discovered that the handwriting of Setauket native Robert Townsend matched the handwriting of letters signed with the alias "Samuel Culper, Jr."

But even as historians slowly unearthed the names of other members of the ring over the next few decades, one remained unknown. Abraham Woodhull ("Samuel Culper, Sr."), the leader of the Culper Ring, referred to this person only as agent 355 (Culper code for *lady*), but his admiration for her was unquestionable. In a letter to Benjamin Tallmadge, Washington's spymaster, Abraham wrote, "I intend to visit 727 [New York] before long and think by the assistance of a 355 [lady] of my acquaintance, shall be able to outwit them all."

Historians suggested all kinds of possibilities for the identity of agent 355, but in recent years, Anna Smith Strong emerged as the most credible candidate. She, unlike the other suggested possibilities for agent 355, was a native of the close-knit Setauket community, like almost all of the other members of the Culper Spy Ring. Her husband was imprisoned on a British prison ship for a significant part of the war, giving her a reason to visit New York frequently—and motivation to resist the British. Her family legend, passed down to the present day, holds that she used petticoats on her laundry line to signal Caleb Brewster, who smuggled intelligence

by boat across Long Island Sound to the mainland. Strong family lore also says that Anna made large orders of goods from New York to give Abraham, and perhaps herself, an excuse to make frequent trips into the city.

The other members of the spy ring mentioned in this book are all historical, and the known details of Anna's life form the basis for the story: her family farm on Setauket, the nighttime intrusion of a British soldier into her home, her husband's imprisonment, and the separation of her children due to the circumstances of the war. The details of Benedict Arnold's attempted betrayal of the American cause are also historical, as is the fact that the Culper Ring played a role in unmasking Arnold, who nearly delivered the newborn America into the hands of the British.

Shortly after the war, George Washington paid a visit to Setauket, where he appears to have visited with members of the Culper Ring at a local pub, possibly to thank them for their wartime service. Selah Strong, Anna's husband, was part of the small group that met with the victorious general. Since Selah was in prison or in hiding on the mainland for most of the war and would not have been able to play much of a part in the spy ring himself, his presence is yet another clue that Anna Strong was, in fact, the mysterious agent 355.

A note on codes: The Culper Code included in the spycraft envelope is based on the real code that the Culper Spy Ring used. Pigpen cipher is another real code system that may have also been used by Revolutionary War spies.

Bibliography

Allen, Thomas B. *George Washington, Spymaster: How the Americans Outspied the British and Won the Revolutionary War.* Washington, DC: National Geographic Children's Books, 2007.

Daigler, Kenneth. *Spies, Patriots, and Traitors: American Intelligence in the Revolutionary War.* New York: Georgetown University Press, 2015.

Ferling, John. *Almost a Miracle: The American Victory in the War of Independence.* New York: Oxford University Press, 2007.

Middlekauff, Robert. *The Glorious Cause: The American Revolution, 1763–1789.* New York: Oxford University Press, 2007.

Rose, Alexander. *Washington's Spies: The Story of America's First Spy Ring.* New York: Bantam, 2006.

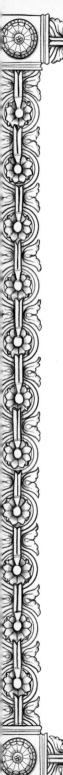

Tyler, Beverly. *A Case for Anna Smith Strong: Her Relationship with the Setauket-Based Culper Spy Ring.* PDF. http://www.threevillagehistoricalsociety. org/wp-content/uploads/2015/01/Hi_2014-131415- ACaseForAnnaSmithStrong.pdf (Accessed 1/12/2018)

Wood, Gordon S. *The American Revolution: A History.* New York: Modern Library Chronicles, 2003.

WAIT!

Have you solved the mystery hidden in this book?

Don't crack this seal until you've cracked the code and discovered Anna's secret!

Answer Key

In order to solve the mystery hidden within this book, you have to use the spy tools included in the envelope.

The vellum sheet has six silhouettes, a line written in pigpen code, and a number of rectangular holes. The pigpen code on the sheet asks "What has Anna hidden?" Throughout the book, there are silhouettes that match those on the vellum sheet. Line up the matching silhouettes, and a word will appear in one of the rectangular holes. To discover the answer to the question, rearrange the words you find to read: "New version of the Culper Code."

The Culper Code and the cipher wheel included in the spy envelope can be used to decode Anna's letter, which raises another question: In which Setauket cove did Anna hide the new code?

To answer this question—and to uncover the proper alignment for the cipher wheel—look closely at the illustrations throughout the book. Many clues must be translated using the Culper Code or pigpen. There are several ways to arrive at the right answer, so you don't have to find every clue in order to solve the mystery.

MAP: The pigpen hidden in the top of the map's frame reads "In the cove with three letters." This indicates that the new version of the Culper Code is hidden in cove one, two, or six.

COPYRIGHT PAGE: The black letters spell out "True Patriots start at one and end with tea." This is a subtle clue for the proper cipher wheel alignment. "Start at one" suggests that the start of the alphabet (the letter A) should be aligned with the number 1. "End with tea" suggests that the end of the alphabet (the letter Z) should be aligned with the letter t. This puts the letter e in line with A and 1, creating the proper alignment: Ae1.

PAGE 13: Look carefully at the King's Proclamation to find another clue to the cipher wheel's alignment, Ae1. The pigpen on the bottom of the note reads "not two," meaning that the new Culper Code is not hidden in cove two.

PAGE 15: The pigpen hidden in the frame divider reads "All Anna's children know which cove." Anna has six children, so this is a clue that the new Culper Code is hidden in cove six. The equation "3x2" on Abraham's gun also points to cove six.

PAGE 17: Place the red acetate (included in the spy envelope) over Anna's sleeve to find Ae1, the cipher wheel alignment.

PAGE 19: The pigpen hidden along the bottom of the ship reads "On water, in air." There are six people in the small boat ("on water") and six flags flying from the ship ("in air"). This indicates cove six. (There are also six cannons on the ship.)

PAGE 20: Use the red acetate to uncover three pieces of Culper Code embedded in this image. Each code redirects to other pages with clues. 364 is code for "longitude," which directs you to the map at the beginning of the book (in case you missed the map's hidden pigpen). 259 is code for "harvest," which leads to the illustration on page 48. 255 is code for "horse," which suggests you should look closely at the illustrations featuring horses throughout the book. The pigpen on the deck reads "Find clothespins," which indicates that the clothespins hidden in the illustrations often contain clues.

PAGE 23: There is a repeating pattern of sixes in the teacup, indicating cove six.

PAGE 26: The pigpen hidden in the fireplace bricks reads "Note the details." Look closely at the rocking chair—there is a repeating pattern of sixes engraved on the back panels.

PAGE 28: Place the red acetate over the fire to reveal a piece of Culper Code on the clothespin-shaped log. 592 is code for "ship," which directs back to the illustration on page 19, in case you missed the clues there.

PAGE 30: Place the red acetate over Nathan Hale's letter to reveal the cipher code's alignment, Ae1.

PAGE 32: There are six handkerchiefs on the clothesline, indicating cove six.

PAGE 33: Anna mentions to Abraham that there are half a dozen coves in Setauket, which establishes that there are six coves where the new code might be hidden.

PAGE 36: There is a repeating motif of threes in this illustration—three people, three apples, three buttons on Abraham's coat. This is a red herring, suggesting that Anna may have hidden the new Culper Code in cove three.

PAGE 38: Place the red acetate over the shopping list to reveal a letter to General Washington. This page also has a subtle clue to the location of the new Culper Code: There are six items to purchase.

PAGE 41: The pigpen code hidden in the basket reads "four." This is a red herring, suggesting cove four.

PAGE 44: The pigpen code at the top of the frame reads "Find the pattern." This refers to the pattern of six strokes that runs along the frame, indicating cove six.

PAGE 46: Place the red acetate over the clothespins to reveal three pieces of Culper Code directing you to other pages with clues. 219 is code for "gun," leading to the illustrations on pages 15 and 26. 106 is code for "cannon," leading to the illustration on page 19. 356 is code for "letter," leading to the illustration on page 44.

PAGE 48: There is a repeating motif of fives in this illustration—five soldiers, five crop rows, five carrots. The pigpen between the crop rows reads "Can it be five?" This is a red herring, suggesting cove five.

PAGE 50: Place the red acetate over the chair to reveal a Culper Code in the clothespin-shaped spindle. 581 is code for "rebellion," redirecting to the King's Proclamation on page 13, in case you missed the clue there.

PAGE 53: The pigpen on the top of the frame reads "Gen Arnold says cove four."

PAGE 56: The cipher alignment key Ae1 is hidden in the curtains. The pigpen along the edge of the wall reads "Beware of traitors." Benedict Arnold was a traitor, which means he can't be trusted. This indicates that the clue on page 53 is a red herring.

PAGE 59: The pigpen hidden along the dirt road reads "Cove marked with an X." This is a subtle clue referring to the letter x at the end of "six."

PAGE 61: Place the red acetate over the lantern to reveal a piece of Culper Code. 479 is code for "party," indicating that there is a clue hidden in the party scene on page 56.

PAGE 67: The cipher alignment key Ae1 is hidden in Anna's coat. Place the red acetate over the clothespin hidden in the barrel to reveal a piece of Culper Code. 313 is code for "instrument," redirecting back to the illustration on page 53.

PAGE 70: There is a repeating motif of fours in this illustration—four soldiers, four buttons on the coats, four rocks. This is a red herring suggesting cove four.

PAGE 73: There are two pieces of Culper Code hidden in the clothespin-shaped fence posts. 703 is code for "wagon," redirecting back to the illustration on page 59. 318 is code for "imprison," redirecting back to the illustration on page 20, where Selah is in chains. The pigpen in the bush reads "Count." There are six soldiers in the yard, indicating cove six.

SOLUTION: Anna hid a revised version of the Culper Code in cove six!

CALEB,
725,

WE ARE GUILTY OF MUCH MISCHIEF IN
682 eli 229 431 380 390 282

ORDER TO PROTECT THE LAND WE LOVE.
439 634 506 625 347 682 348.

MY LAST EFFORT WAS TO DELIVER THE
ns meuv ijjqlv yeu vq himcxil vbi

REVISED VERSION OF THE CULPER CODE
lixcuih xilucqp qj vbi gwmril gqhi

TO ONE OF THE SETAUKET COVES.
vq qpi qj vbi uivewoiv gqxiu.

CAN YOU GET THIS COPY SAFELY TO
gep sqw aiv vbcu gqrs uejims vq

GENERAL WASHINGTON?
aipilem yeubcpavqp?

BE SAFE,
fi ueji,

ANNA
eppe

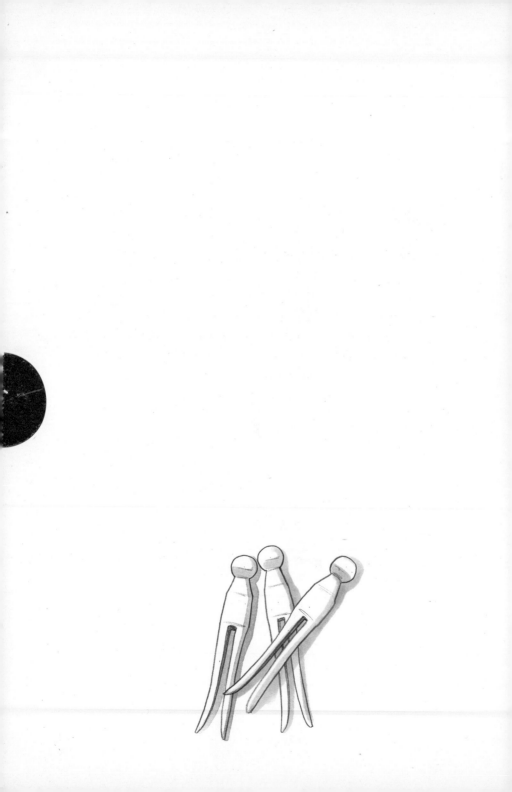